Praise for *Everyday G*

"Paul Tripp's *Everyday Gospel* is a wonder. It's brilliantly written, clear, concise, Christ-exalting, true to God's word, enriching to the mind, encouraging to the heart, and overflowing with gospel grace. Every paragraph has the ring of truth. If you want a daily dose of God's life-giving wisdom and kindness, this book is for you."
    Randy Alcorn, author, *Heaven*; *If God Is Good*; and *The Treasure Principle*

"This deeply nourishing devotional reader gives us what we have all come to expect and gratefully receive from Paul Tripp: wise bridge-building from the depths of Scripture before us to the depths of our hearts within us, always flavored with the hope of the gospel. This will be a heartening and life-giving journey for any who receive Tripp's guidance through the Scripture each day."
    Dane Ortlund, Senior Pastor, Naperville Presbyterian Church, Naperville, Illinois; author, *Gentle and Lowly: The Heart of Christ for Sinners and Sufferers*

"*New Morning Mercies* has been on our living room book table for years, and *Everyday Gospel* will soon be joining it. I encourage you to consider doing likewise."
    Tim Challies, author, *Seasons of Sorrow*

"I need the gospel every day—not just a glimpse of it but the full depth and beauty revealed throughout all of Scripture. That's why I love this devotional. Paul Tripp brings the eternal truths of the gospel straight to the heart and shows us how to live in light of them. I hope many will use this resource and learn to walk in the good news of Jesus every single day."
    Jeremy Treat, Pastor for Preaching and Vision, Reality LA, Los Angeles, California; Professor of Theology, Biola University; author, *The Crucified King*; *Seek First*; and *The Atonement*

EVERYDAY GOSPEL

Christmas Devotional

EVERYDAY GOSPEL

Christmas Devotional

PAUL DAVID TRIPP

WHEATON, ILLINOIS · ESV.ORG

Everyday Gospel Christmas Devotional

© 2025 by Paul David Tripp

Published by Crossway
        1300 Crescent Street
        Wheaton, Illinois 60187

All rights reserved. No part of this publication may be reproduced, stored in a retrieval system, or transmitted in any form by any means, electronic, mechanical, photocopy, recording, or otherwise, without the prior permission of the publisher, except as provided for by USA copyright law. Crossway® is a registered trademark in the United States of America.

Cover design and illustration: Jordan Singer

First printing 2025

Printed in the United States of America

Scripture quotations are from the ESV® Bible (The Holy Bible, English Standard Version®), © 2001 by Crossway, a publishing ministry of Good News Publishers. Used by permission. All rights reserved. The ESV text may not be quoted in any publication made available to the public by a Creative Commons license. The ESV may not be translated in whole or in part into any other language.

Paperback ISBN: 979-8-8749-0793-8
ePub ISBN: 979-8-8749-0795-2
PDF ISBN: 979-8-8749-0793-8

Library of Congress Control Number: 2025938964

Crossway is a publishing ministry of Good News Publishers.

LB		35	34	33	32	31	30	29	28	27	26	25
15	14	13	12	11	10	9	8	7	6	5	4	3	2	1

CONTENTS

December 1   *Genesis 3:14–21*
December 2   *Genesis 21:1–7*
December 3   *Exodus 4:1–17*
December 4   *Ruth 4:13–22*
December 5   *2 Kings 23:1–14*
December 6   *Esther 4:1–17*
December 7   *Job 33:12–33*
December 8   *Psalm 42:1–11*
December 9   *Psalm 89:1–18*
December 10 *Isaiah 9:1–7*
December 11 *Jeremiah 23:1–8*
December 12 *Ezekiel 25:1–17*
December 13 *Ezekiel 34:11–31*
December 14 *Daniel 7:1–18*
December 15 *Matthew 2:1–12*
December 16 *Matthew 3:1–17*
December 17 *Matthew 20:20–28*
December 18 *Luke 1:26–55*
December 19 *Luke 2:22–38*
December 20 *John 1:1–18*
December 21 *John 3:1–21*
December 22 *John 20:24–31*
December 23 *Philippians 2:1–18*
December 24 *Hebrews 1:1–14*
December 25 *Revelation 12:1–17*

INTRODUCTION

I love Christmas. You would struggle to find someone as enthusiastic as Paul Tripp about all the festivities that fill a typical December calendar. I love baking Christmas cookies, decorating Christmas trees (we have three!), attending Christmas concerts, and shopping for Christmas gifts for loved ones.

Yet simultaneously this season makes me sad. The chaotic cultural emphasis on Christmas has flipped the true meaning of Advent upside down. What should be a celebratory and reflective season, in which we rejoice in the incarnation of the Creator and surrender worshipfully to his lordship, has become a frenzied pursuit of manufactured delights. We have "exchanged the truth about God for a lie and worshiped and served the creature rather than the Creator" (Rom. 1:25).

Particularly for our children, the lie being actively promoted is how their lives will be made infinitely better by possessing a particular manufactured item. For families seeking to focus the wonder of their kids away from the next trinket or toy and toward the wonder of the coming of our great Lord and Savior, Christmas has become a parent's nightmare and a retailer's dream.

So I humbly present to you this resource that may help in the battle for your family's attention. The *Everyday Gospel Christmas Devotional* is a twenty-five-day Bible reading plan with my commentary that will take you from December 1 through Christmas morning. My prayer is that the glory of the incarnation of the Creator would become far more attractive than the manufactured delights of Christmas so that we truly come and adore Christ the Lord, as the classic hymn we sing declares.

Why don't you and your family and your church journey with me for the first twenty-five days of December, walking through the garden of wisdom, truth, and grace that God prepared for us when he guided the recording and preservation of his word? As you read each of these Christmas entries, remember that the Bible is a story with a singular focus: to celebrate Jesus.

Nothing could be more important this December than spending daily time in the word, rejoicing that the Word became flesh and made his dwelling among us (John 1:14). He is our hope and the reason for this Advent season!

PAUL DAVID TRIPP

DECEMBER 1
GENESIS 3:14–21

God doesn't wait too long to reveal the biblical narrative. The whole story is in compressed form in the first three chapters of Genesis.

Genesis begins with the most brilliant, mind-bending, and heart-engaging introduction to a book ever written. God knows how much we need the creation-to-destiny themes of the biblical narrative in order to make sense of our lives, so he lovingly gives us those dominant themes right up front. The beginning of the Bible is wonderful, awe-inspiring, heartbreaking, cautionary, and hope-instilling all at once. Since God created us to be meaning-makers, he immediately presents us with the wonderful and awful realities that we need to understand in order to make proper sense of who we are and what life is really all about.

The opening chapters of Genesis have three foundational themes.

1. *In the center of all that is, there is a God of incalculable glory.* The first four words of Genesis say it all: "In the beginning, God." Here is the ultimate fact through which every other fact of life is properly understood. There is a God. He is the Creator of everything that exists. He is glorious in power, authority, wisdom, sovereignty, and love. Since we are his creatures, knowing him, loving him, worshiping him, and obeying him define our identity, meaning, and purpose as human beings.

2. *Sin is the ultimate human tragedy. Its legacy is destruction and death.* Genesis 3 is the most horrible, saddest chapter ever written. In an act of outrageous rebellion, Adam and Eve stepped over God's wise and holy boundaries, ushering in a horrible plague of iniquity that would infect every human heart. Because sin is a matter of the heart, we are confronted in this narrative with the fact

that our greatest problem in life is us, and because it is, we have no power to escape it on our own.

3. *A Savior will come, crush the power of evil, and provide redemption for his people.* The first three chapters of the Bible end with glorious hope. We are encouraged to understand that sin is not ultimate—God is. And he had already set a plan in motion to do for us, through the Son to come, what we could not do for ourselves. A second Adam would come, defeat temptation, crush the evil one, and restore us to God. As soon as sin rears its ugly face, redemption is promised. What grace!

It really is true that three themes course through God's amazing word: *creation, fall,* and *redemption.* They form the lens through which we can look at and understand everything in our lives. What a sweet grace it is that immediately in his word God makes himself known, alerts us to the tragedy of sin, and welcomes us into the hope of the saving grace to be found in the seed of the woman, his Son, the Lord Jesus. We are left with the riches of a single truth that is the core of everything the Bible has to say: Because God is a God of grace, mercy really will triumph over judgment.

REFLECTION

How might reflecting on the three themes of creation, fall, and redemption help to prepare you for the celebration of Christ's first advent and to fill you with anticipation of his second coming?

PRAYER

Creator God, I praise you for the glory and beauty of this world that you have made. And I praise you for the glory and beauty of your Son, who has come to rescue us from our sin, which has so marred this world. Thank you that he has accomplished all that the first Adam could not. In Jesus's name, amen.

DECEMBER 2
GENESIS 21:1–7

So much of our fear, discouragement, anxiety, and worry is the result of underestimating what God is willing and able to do.

Rest and patience of heart are not found in figuring out what is going on or conjuring up in our minds how in the world God is going to do what he's promised us that he would do. Rest and patience of heart are found in trusting the one who has it all figured out and knows exactly how he will accomplish what he has promised he will do. We are limited human beings. We all carry spiritual, mental, emotional, and physical limits with us wherever we go. We are all limited in righteousness, wisdom, and strength. Unless we are resting in the presence and power of the Lord, we will evaluate situations from the perspective of our many limits. This means that what appears to us to be completely impossible is quite possible with our Lord. His strength, his understanding, his compassion, and his grace are infinite.

Sometimes we make good-hearted promises that later we realize we are unable to keep. We know things need to get done, but we do not have the power or the wisdom to do them. There is nothing that God has promised to do or that we need him to do that he is unable to do. Nothing. We have every blessing that we have because he has the power to control the forces of nature, the events of history, and the unfolding of situations. Not only has he created everything, but everything he has created does his bidding. He is magnificent, almighty in power and wisdom. He can and will do what he has promised to do.

So God was not limited at all by Abraham or Sarah's age, any more than any other human limit would inhibit his ability to do what he has promised he would do. Genesis 21:1–7 records the birth of the promised son, Isaac. It also records that Abraham was one hundred. That's right: one hundred years old—and Sarah was in her nineties. The God who is the Lord of heaven and earth is also Lord of the womb of an old woman, and he can do through it what he has promised to do. He is the Lord. He is not limited by our weaknesses.

When I read the story of Abraham and Sarah's long wait for a promised son, I think of another Son that was promised. The hope of the world rested on the shoulders of this promised Son, but as century followed century, it seemed as though this Son would never come. But one night in a stable in Bethlehem, to a lowly carpenter and his wife the promised Messiah came. Nothing in all of those centuries that had passed was able to stop the promise of God. Jesus, Son of Man, Son of God, the Lamb, the Savior was born at just the right time to provide justification, reconciliation, forgiveness, and new life to all who believe. God's promises are not limited by human weakness or the passage of time. Don't give way to fear; God will do what he has promised to do.

---- REFLECTION ----

Besides the birth of a promised son, what other promises of God do we see fulfilled in the coming and birth of Jesus in Bethlehem?

---- PRAYER ----

Lord, I stand in awe of your almighty power and wisdom. Thank you for using these attributes for your own glory and the good of your people—especially in sending the promised Messiah, your Son, the Lord Jesus. I praise you in his name, amen.

DECEMBER 3

EXODUS 4:1–17

*God calls us to represent him in this fallen world
not because we are able but because he is.*

Moses is living as a fugitive in the wilderness because he had killed an Egyptian taskmaster. But God has plans for Moses. God has chosen Moses to be his tool of redeeming power. He is calling Moses back to Egypt to stand before Pharaoh and demand the release of all the Israelite slaves (Ex. 3). Put yourself in Moses's shoes. Would you be excited about going back to Egypt? Would you feel confident to stand before the most powerful ruler of the world and demand that he free a group of people that was a major element in his nation's economic engine?

In this moment, Moses does what we often do when God calls us. We compare our natural gifts and abilities to the size of the task, to gauge whether we are capable of doing what God has called us to do. God doesn't call us because we have, in ourselves, everything we need to accomplish what he's calling us to do. No, he calls weak and broken people to do huge and important things because he is able. He is with us, and he empowers us to do what he wills for us to do. Every one of God's commands is accompanied by his empowering grace. Exodus 4 records how God demonstrates his power to fearful Moses to assure him that he will go down to Egypt and stand before Pharaoh not in his own power, but in the awesome power of the King of kings and the Lord of lords.

But Moses isn't easy to convince. God says, "I can even turn the waters of the Nile into blood as a demonstration of my power before Pharaoh" (see Ex. 4:9). Moses responds, "I am not eloquent . . . I am slow of speech and of tongue" (4:10). God says, "Moses, I created your mouth. I am the Lord, and I will go with you and teach you what to say" (see Ex. 4:11–12). I love this picture of the patience of the Lord, working to take Moses's eyes off himself and onto the majestic power of his God. Sadly, Moses responds, "Oh, my Lord, please send someone else" (4:13).

God calls husbands, wives, parents, workers, neighbors, friends, university students, the young, and the old to represent him in this dark world. He calls average people to do things that are anything but average. Is there a place in your life where you are responding, "Oh, Lord, please send someone else"?

Another person was later called to provide redemption from slavery, this time the slavery to sin. His name was Jesus. His call was not just to speak but to die, so that we could know freedom as the children of God. It is in the power of his redeeming grace that we are able to say yes to the call of God, because we know Jesus's death and resurrection guarantee just the grace we need to do what God has called us to do at just the time we need it. In him weak and fearful people are made able, and that's very good news.

---— REFLECTION ---—

How does Jesus free us from our slavery to sin and death? In what ways did the Father prepare and equip Jesus for that task?

---— PRAYER ---—

Dear God, help me to represent you well. Allow others to see your love and glory as I serve you. And thank you for sending one to represent me perfectly, my Savior, Jesus, through whom I come to you now. Amen.

DECEMBER 4
RUTH 4:13–22

Often when God seems absent in moments of hardship, he is actually exercising his sovereignty to deliver good gifts of grace to his children.

We have all been through tough moments of suffering when we wonder where God is and are confused about what he is doing. If you read through the biblical narrative, you will soon have to let go of the conclusion that hardship means God is absent, distant, uninvolved, or uncaring. Behind dark clouds of difficulty is a God who is actively working for the good of his children. God regularly takes his children places they never would have planned to go in order to produce in and through them things they never could have produced on their own. It's important to recognize that the workings of God's grace aren't always predictable or comfortable. Often when we think grace has passed us by, God's grace is at work, just not in the way we expect.

The book of Ruth, one of the greatest biblical stories, contains a compelling and beautiful substory. On the surface Ruth is a beautiful love story, and one of the few biblical stories with women as main characters. But there is a deeper, more significant love story in the book of Ruth. It is the story of God's unshakable, unstoppable love for his children. This story of human hardship and human love is also God's assurance that he will exercise his wisdom and his sovereignty, he will remember his covenant promises, he will be faithful, and, through hardship, he will deliver gifts of kindness and grace to his own. Although the story of Naomi, Ruth, and Boaz is compelling, it is the Lord who takes center stage. Through the vehicles of hardship and human love, God establishes the direction of the rest of the redemptive story.

At the end of the story, Ruth and Boaz have a son. We read, "Then Naomi took the child and laid him on her lap and became his nurse. And the women of the neighborhood gave him a name, saying, 'A son has been born to Naomi.' They named him Obed. He was the father of Jesse, the father of David" (Ruth 4:16–17). These words give us a sense of what this story has been about all along. God doesn't just deliver Ruth and unite her to Boaz, but he delivers to this family a son. This son, Obed, will have a son, Jesse, and Jesse will have a son, David, and ultimately out of David will come a son, the Son of David, Jesus. Through this little story of hardship and love, God sets things in place to deliver something that is anything but little: the ultimate promise, the gift of gifts, the Savior, Jesus Christ, through whom God's redeeming love will flow.

God will work and continue to work his redeeming plan until that plan is complete; this is the ultimate story behind every other story. Remember that it is at the intersection of God's sovereignty and his grace that life and hope are to be found.

---—— REFLECTION ——---

In what ways does God work through the lives of Mary and Joseph to bring his redemptive plan to fruition in the birth and life of Jesus?

---—— PRAYER ——---

Lord of Heaven, your love is unshakable, unstoppable. I praise you that you have injected daily reminders of this great truth into my life. Keep me from ever losing sight of your covenant commitment to your people—rooted in your faithful and eternal love for your Son, through whom I pray, amen.

DECEMBER 5
2 KINGS 23:1–14

No matter how bad and spiritually dark things may seem, don't ever stop praying for moral and spiritual revival.

Just when you get to the point where you want to stop reading the Old Testament because it has become so dark and discouraging, out of the darkness rises young King Josiah. Rather than reading about more idolatry, infanticide, desecration of the house of the Lord, or consultations with fortune tellers and necromancers, you find real spiritual revival. In the darkness a bright light shines through the moral commitments of a young and godly king. One of the first things this king does is to lead the children of Judah in a revival service. He leads the people in a covenant-renewing ceremony, in which they again vow their allegiance to the covenant of the Lord. Josiah then leads his people in a wholesale destruction of idol high places and idol practices. Out of utter spiritual darkness comes this moment of spiritual revival. God's law is observed and his covenant renewed. It had not seemed that this would be the next chapter for the people of Israel; and, yes, God would later raise up Babylon to purge his people and call them back to himself. But the beauty of this moment of revival should not be diminished.

A rallying cry for the Protestant Reformers was the Latin phrase *post tenebras lux* ("after darkness, light"). Spiritual darkness had blanketed Europe, and the light and glory of the grace of the gospel of Jesus Christ seemed like a tiny flickering flame. But out of the darkness God raised up Martin Luther, John Calvin, and other gospel lights. The flames of the gospel burned bright in Europe, spread throughout the world, and burn brightly still today.

Between the "already" and the "not yet," *post tenebras lux* is and has always been the hope of God's people. This hope is rooted in the goodness, holiness, power, promises, and grace of God. It is about holding on to the belief that God will not let his grace die, that he will not let his plan fade away, and that he will keep every one of the promises he has made.

The birth of Jesus was a monumental *post tenebras lux* moment. He came into this dark world as the light shining in darkness (John 1:5). Jesus is the eternal light, the eternal torch that nothing or no one could ever extinguish. He shines into the hearts of all who put their trust in him.

The world might seem dark to you today, but another *post tenebras lux* moment is coming, when the light will come for his own, ushering them into his final kingdom of light, life, peace, and righteousness forever. Darkness will not ultimately defeat the light, and so, with the same hope as the Reformers, we say *post tenebras lux*.

---— REFLECTION ———

How has Jesus brought light into this world? How has he brought light into your life specifically?

———— PRAYER ————

Heavenly Father, I rest in the fact that your grace is everlasting. You are the sovereign King of this universe who will not let his plan fade away, who will always be faithful to his promises. Help me to rest in these truths. May I grow in patience, not in anxiety. Cause me to rest in Jesus, my shepherd and King. In his name I pray, amen.

DECEMBER 6
ESTHER 4:1–17

The God who works in the light also works in the shadows. If you do not see his hand, don't conclude that he isn't working.

When I counseled people, they would tell me their stories. Often they would recount their lives and express no sense of God's presence or influence. I found this jarring. So I would act as a tour guide, walking them back through their stories and pointing out evidence of God's presence, care, provision, and grace. Sometimes God works in the bright light. His hand is obvious, and his care is clear. But sometimes it is hard to "see" God. In these moments, it's tempting to wonder whether he is near and whether he is doing anything. So it is important to understand that the God who works in the light also works in the shadows. His sovereign power and redeeming care are not always clear, but we ought not think he is absent, distant, inactive, or uncaring. God never forsakes his own, and he never fails to deliver what he has promised. The assumption that we can't see evidence of his presence or care does not mean he is not present and at work.

I think one of the reasons the book of Esther is in the Bible is to teach us this lesson. Esther is one book of the Bible that does not mention God's name. This has troubled many people, but it shouldn't because there is evidence of God's power, presence, and care for his people throughout this little Old Testament book. God works in the shadows to cause Esther to rise to prominence in order to preserve his people. In so doing, God gives hope to the world, because out of those people the Savior would come and ultimately make new again everything broken by sin. Without Esther, the Jewish people would have been destroyed, and there would have been no birth of the Messiah in Bethlehem, no righteous life of Jesus, no substitutionary death, no victorious resurrection, and no ascension to the Father to intercede for his own. The world would have been trapped in sin and doomed with no hope.

The amazing outcome of the story of Esther cannot and should not be attributed to human initiative, wisdom, and ingenuity alone. Behind everything, God is controlling circumstances, working in people's hearts, and determining outcomes. We should be thankful for Mordecai and Esther, but God is the ultimate hero of this portion of Scripture. His providential care guarantees that his people and his work of redemption will have an eternal and glorious future.

You may not always see God's hand, but you can rest assured that your Lord never ceases working for your good and his glory. Remember that the God who is active in the light is just as active in the shadows. Even though his name might not appear to be plastered all over your story, he is with you, in you, and for you—and that is reason to rest in his care and give yourself to his work.

REFLECTION

Does God work now in hidden or surprising ways? How have you seen evidence of this in your own life or your own church?

PRAYER

O great God, I know that you are always working. Although I do not always see your hand, help me to trust in you nevertheless. Show me how you have been working in the past. Thank you for working out all things for your glory and my good, especially through the salvation of mankind through Christ, in whose name I pray, amen.

DECEMBER 7
JOB 33:12-33

Remember that God's primary concern is not earthly comfort but eternal rescue.

Sometimes we struggle with God not because he is unloving or unfaithful (he never is!) but because our values don't match his. When we read through the biblical narrative, we realize that God's primary agenda is not that we would achieve a comfortable and pleasurable life between the "already" and the "not yet." Think about what makes you frustrated, irritated, disappointed, or sad. Think about what makes you happy, satisfied, or content. What causes these feelings? How many of your joys and sorrows have anything whatsoever to do with the kingdom and purposes of God? How often do you mourn your lack of conformity to his perfect and wise will? How often do you celebrate the outpouring of daily grace? How often are you grieved because your heart still wanders? How often are you grateful that God meets you every day with rescuing and restraining mercies? Many of us don't need a disaster in order to feel frustration and disappointment; no, a flat tire or missing the subway on the way to work can wreck our day.

We experience sturdy joy—the kind that does not rise or fall with our circumstances—when what we want most for ourselves matches what God wants for us. But if what we want is not the thing that God wants most for us, then we are living at cross-purposes with him and struggle to see him as kind, good, faithful, and loving. And when we begin to question the goodness of God, we stop going to him for help and instead we seek help only from those who we think are good and trustworthy.

Elihu entered the scene of this great moral drama in Job 32 to correct Job's three counselors. Although in some ways Elihu is as legalistic as Job's other friends, he has moments of wisdom and insight:

> God speaks in one way,
>   and in two, though man does not perceive it.
> In a dream, in a vision of the night,
>   when deep sleep falls on men,
>   while they slumber on their beds,
> then he opens the ears of men
>   and terrifies them with warnings,
> that he may turn man aside from his deed
>   and conceal pride from a man;
> he keeps back his soul from the pit,
>   his life from perishing by the sword. (Job 33:14–18)

Elihu is on to something. Why do we fail to see God? Why do we fail to hear his words? It is not because he has forsaken us. It is not because he is silent. It is because while we are worrying about why our lives have been so hard, God is working on something much more significant and glorious than the comforts of the moment. With wisdom, faithfulness, and rescuing grace, he is securing our eternal rescue. And that is a reason to celebrate!

──────────── REFLECTION ────────────

How can knowing that God is securing our eternal rescue lead to sturdy joy amid the trials of this life?

──────────── PRAYER ────────────

Eternal God, shape my goals and desires to match yours. Grant happiness, satisfaction, and contentment in your holy will for this world and for my life. Replace my doubt with a humble reliance on your perfect sovereignty. Give me the peace of Jesus, in whose name I pray, amen.

DECEMBER 8

PSALM 42:1–11

*Your body always moves toward what
your heart has been longing for.*

If I could eavesdrop on the longings of your heart, what would I hear? Maybe you're single and long for the lifelong companionship of marriage. Maybe you have a job, but what you long for is a satisfying career. Perhaps in the midst of extended family chaos, you long for the sweetness of family peace. Maybe you're sick and long for physical health and strength. Perhaps you long for enough money to pay your bills or to afford a dependable car. You may be a student who longs for success in your upcoming exams. Our hearts are never free from longing and, as the Bible reveals, our bodies follow after the longings of our hearts.

Psalm 42 is about the beautiful and life-giving longing that God designed to rule our hearts and shape how we live. What is this longing? It is longing for God himself. Longing for God involves longing for his presence, his fellowship, his wise rule, his rescuing grace, and the gathering of others who long for him as well. But in order to long for God, grace must first inspire and empower that longing. At the center of what sin is and does is a longing to *be* God. This desire goes all the way back to the fall in the garden of Eden. And because we are born in sin, we are born with idolatrous longing. Rather than naturally longing for God, we long for his position, power, and rule. We all need grace to rescue us from idolatry of self, so that our hearts may reach up to the one who first reached down to us.

Psalm 42 is both convicting and encouraging:

As a deer pants for flowing streams,
   so pants my soul for you, O God.

My soul thirsts for God,
    for the living God.
When shall I come and appear before God?
My tears have been my food
    day and night,
while they say to me all the day long,
    "Where is your God?"
These things I remember,
    as I pour out my soul:
how I would go with the throng
    and lead them in procession to the house of God
with glad shouts and songs of praise,
    a multitude keeping festival. (Ps. 42:1–4)

Be honest today: Do you hunger after and long for God? Are you like a parched deer, panting for water? Does longing for God propel your devotional life, your relationships, and your participation in public worship? Longing for God will always produce love for the people of God and joyful participation in the public worship of God.

If you lack that longing, remember that Jesus came to restore what sin robbed you of. Pray that God would place a longing for him in your heart. God delights when his people long for him, so he delights in answering our prayers for that longing.

---- REFLECTION ----

In what ways might reflecting anew on the Christmas story deepen your hunger and longing for God?

---- PRAYER ----

Precious Savior, my soul is often cast down. But I rest in your steadfast love. And may I long for it more and more. Thank you for comforting me with your presence, night and day. In Jesus's name, amen.

DECEMBER 9

PSALM 89:1–18

Where does your mind go and your heart
run when life doesn't make sense?

I counseled a woman who had enjoyed a wonderful life. She and her successful husband had two wonderful children. She attended a good church and was surrounded by a group of devoted friends. But in an act of unfaithfulness and betrayal, her husband forsook her, and she lost everything. After she realized the extent of her loss, she had no life in her eyes, no spring in her step, and no hope in her heart. She was burdened by the uncertainty of her future. Where would she live? How would she survive? I couldn't answer all of her questions, but I knew one thing: She was not without hope. I told her that even in the face of all the grief and loss, she would stand. I told her this not because she was strong, wise, and capable, but because the most important person in her life, the one who was near to her and who would give her the grace to continue, had not forsaken her. We talked about the rock of hope that was hers in the steadfast love of the Lord, a love that never fails. I did my best to help her see that his steadfast love was as real as all of the loss that had so devastated her. Then we talked about the decisions she needed to make to move forward in her new circumstances.

When our comfortable plans for our life come crashing down, God can seem distant and inactive. Psalm 89 paints a picture for us of two colliding realities. It first celebrates God's steadfast love:

> I will sing of the steadfast love of the LORD forever;
>   with my mouth I will make known your faithfulness to all
>   generations. (Ps. 89:1)

This is the rock of hope for believers of all generations, for Old Testament Israelites as well as people in the pews in Chicago. We all experience the bright mountain peaks and dark valleys of life. Things happen that make us think life is over. In our trouble, we can be tempted to think that God has withdrawn his presence and his promises. But nothing can break his commitment to love his own.

When we read the first verse of this psalm, we might think that it's going to be a happy psalm, but it's not. Psalm 89 is a lament. It was written in a moment when it seemed as though God had turned his back on his children, rejecting them and withdrawing his love. But his discipline in the face of their sin was not a sign that he had withdrawn his love.

The surest indication of the steadfast love of the Lord is the birth, life, death, and resurrection of Jesus. His sacrifice assures us that our sin will not cause God to withdraw the grace of his love. Today, in your trouble, remember where your hope is found: in the steadfast love of the Lord. That love is forever.

―――――――――――――― REFLECTION ――――――――――――――

How is the birth of Christ an indication of his steadfast love? How has he made that love evident in your own life?

―――――――――――――――― PRAYER ――――――――――――――――

O precious Lord, may I never lose sight of your precious love! Who in the skies can be compared to you? Who is mighty as you are, O Lord, with your faithfulness all around you? Thank you for surrounding me with that faithfulness, and especially for lifting up the head of your anointed, Jesus Christ, to resurrection life, which is my hope of eternal blessing. I thank you for all of your promises that are fulfilled in Jesus, through whom I pray, amen.

DECEMBER 10
ISAIAH 9:1–7

Jesus is the grace of God come to earth.

Once on a speaking trip, I stayed at the home of a wealthy family. One room featured a wall full of portraits of past generations of family members. My host explained to me that, in the days before the camera, itinerant painters would travel from city to city in search of well-to-do clients to sit for a portrait. Since painting a portrait takes time, the painter would typically live with the family, in a guesthouse or room, until the painting was complete. In so doing, the painter would get to know the family, particularly the person he was painting. Good painters were known for their ability to capture the essence of the lifestyle, personality, position, and work of their subjects.

If you were to "paint" a verbal picture of Jesus, what words would you use to capture who he is, what he came to do, and what he continues to do in and for those who put their trust in him? It may surprise you, but one of the most beautiful and best-known verbal portraits of Jesus is found not in the New Testament Gospels or Epistles, but rather in the beginning of one of the Old Testament Prophets. For generations, students of the Bible have wondered at, meditated on, and attempted to understand the meaning and implication of the words of this portrait. Perhaps you have already figured out that I am referring to the picture of Jesus painted by Isaiah:

> To us a child is born,
>   to us a son is given;
> and the government shall be upon his shoulder,
>   and his name shall be called
> Wonderful Counselor, Mighty God,
>   Everlasting Father, Prince of Peace.

> Of the increase of his government and of peace
>   there will be no end,
> on the throne of David and over his kingdom,
>   to establish it and to uphold it
> with justice and with righteousness
>   from this time forth and forevermore.
> The zeal of the Lord of hosts will do this. (Isa. 9:6–7)

Jesus is everything Isaiah depicted. Jesus is our source of wisdom, the power by which sin is defeated, the one who adopts us into the family of God forever, and the means by which we have peace with God and with one another. And his kingdom of peace and righteousness will never end. He is the hero at the center of God's plan of redeeming grace, and nothing will impede God's zeal to complete his plan.

It is right to say that in Jesus you find everything you need in order to be what you were meant to be, to do what God designed you to do, and to enjoy life as God meant for you to enjoy it. Jesus is life. Jesus is hope. Jesus is the grace of God. We will spend eternity worshiping and celebrating him. Why not start now?

REFLECTION

Does your celebration of Christmas fill you with anticipation of Jesus's future kingdom of peace and righteousness? Why or why not?

PRAYER

Dear Jesus, I bow in humble adoration of you, my Savior and King. You are indeed a Wonderful Counselor and the Prince of Peace. And you are Mighty God and Everlasting Father! I praise your justice and your righteousness. Your rule is perfect and will extend forever. Thank you for subduing me to yourself and granting me a place in your eternal kingdom. In your name, amen.

DECEMBER 11
JEREMIAH 23:1–8

We have no righteousness of our own; therefore,
we place our hope in the presence and reign
of the perfectly righteous one, Jesus.

Are you tired of another day of devastating news about some horrible thing happening somewhere in the world? Does your battle to cobble together a marriage of unity, understanding, and love discourage you? Are you exhausted by friendship hassles and family drama? Are you sick of hearing about the power of corrupt politicians or failed church leaders? Does your struggle to parent your children get you down? Does the state of the surrounding culture make you weary? Are you tired of the pain and loss around you? Do you look at these things and wonder what can be done? Sometimes it seems as though there's more darkness than light in our world. Sometimes we find ourselves wondering where the true, wise, and moral leaders are. Often we wonder whether there's anything that can be done to right the course.

Into the darkest of days in the time of the prophets, when it seemed as though things were about as bad as they could get and the end of the people of God was near, Jeremiah delivered words of hope. These words were not about human wisdom, intervention, or solutions. When it comes to eradicating evil and setting the human community on a new course, human wisdom, strength, and righteousness fall short. This does not mean we shouldn't fight for what is right or fight against what is wrong, but it does mean we are not the hope that we need. This is why the words of hope in the Old Testament—promises of what is to come—are so important. They speak comfort into sad and tired hearts:

Behold, the days are coming, declares the LORD, when I will raise up for David a righteous Branch, and he shall reign as king and deal wisely, and shall execute justice and righteousness in the land. In his days Judah will be saved, and Israel will dwell securely. And this is the name by which he will be called: "The LORD is our righteousness." (Jer. 23:5–6)

You may be thinking, "How do these words comfort us? Aren't they the promise of a better earthly king for the children of Israel?" The New Testament writers understood these words to be specifically about and fulfilled by Jesus alone (see Matt. 2:2; Luke 1:32; 19:38; John 1:49). Ultimately there is only one solution to the many things that break our hearts and complicate our lives: It is the reign of the risen and ascended King Jesus. The righteous Branch has come and is now sitting at the right hand of the Father. His reign guarantees the final defeat of evil and the ushering in of a kingdom of righteousness and peace forever. In the midst of all the bad news that seems to flood into our lives every day, this is very good news. There is a righteous Branch, his will shall be done, and the scourge of evil will end forever.

―――――――― REFLECTION ――――――――

Where in your life or world do you see the need for a righteous Branch to come and rule? How does the hope of his coming empower you to face those areas?

―――――――― PRAYER ――――――――

I praise you, King Jesus! You are the righteous Branch, promised of old. You have defeated evil and are ushering in a realm of righteousness and peace! I extol your perfect rule and majestic reign over all things. May I rest secure in your everlasting kingdom. In your name I pray, amen.

DECEMBER 12
EZEKIEL 25:1–17

Life on this side of eternity is one constant glory war.

I saw a change in my friend. He had once been a champion of the gospel. It was the fire in his belly, the passion that constantly motivated him. But now he was different. It hadn't happened all at once, but his ministry had changed. It had been all about his Savior, but now it was all about him. He seemed to have fallen into the lure of his own notoriety. He clearly loved being the center of attention. He liked being surrounded by his fans. He loved hanging around with the "cool kids." He was still in ministry and still doing ministry things, but the glory-focus had radically shifted. Whether he knew it or not, the glory that excited him was not the glory of his Savior. He was obsessed with his own glory, and it would be his undoing.

You and I were hardwired by God for glory. We are attracted to glorious things. That's why we love a great meal, an overtime championship game, a beautiful dress, a dramatic movie, or a multihued sunset. God has packed his world full of glorious things and given us the ability to take in those glories. But every glorious thing God has created points to *his* glorious glory. We were never intended to live for our own glory or some created glory. Our glory orientation should drive us to the Lord, so that his glory would finally satisfy the glory hunger in our hearts.

Sin causes us to search for glory satisfaction outside of our Creator, but God will not share his glory with another. God is jealous for his glory to be the one glory that captures our hearts, and this should shape the way that we live. His holy jealousy for his glory is clearly communicated in a single statement repeated in Ezekiel 25–26: "Then you [or they] will know that I am the Lord"

(Ezek. 25:7, 11, 17; 26:6). God is pronouncing judgment on the nations that surround Israel. He exercises his holy justice so that these nations will know that he is the Lord. God exercises his power for his own glory.

Does this bother you? It is wrong to live for your own glory because, as a creature, you belong to the one who made you. You exist by his will and for his purpose. But God is not like you. He reigns in glorious majesty over everything and everyone he has created. His zeal for his own glory is the hope of the universe. It is in living for his glory that we are rescued from our bondage to our own glory, a glory that will never satisfy our hearts.

Only by the power of God's delivering grace are we liberated from our bondage to the glories of creation to find our hope, life, and satisfaction in living for the glory of our Maker. In 2 Corinthians 5:15, the apostle Paul reminds us that we find that grace in the person and work of Jesus. He came so that we would live no longer for ourselves "but for him who for [our] sake died and was raised."

REFLECTION

How was the glory of God revealed in the birth of Jesus? How should that impact your worship this Christmas season?

PRAYER

Lord, help me to live for your glory. Rescue me from the bondage of my own glory, which will not satisfy. I thank you for being my hope, my life, and my satisfaction. I praise the name of Jesus, the one who died and was raised for my sake. May I live for his eternal glory alone, even as I pray in his name, amen.

DECEMBER 13
EZEKIEL 34:11-31

*It is a good thing that our lives are controlled
not by failed human shepherds, but by the
good shepherd, who will never fail.*

After prophesying against the wicked leaders of Israel, Ezekiel brings God's children promises of a faithful good shepherd:

> Therefore, thus says the Lord God to them: Behold, I, I myself will judge between the fat sheep and the lean sheep. Because you push with side and shoulder, and thrust at all the weak with your horns, till you have scattered them abroad, I will rescue my flock; they shall no longer be a prey. And I will judge between sheep and sheep. And I will set up over them one shepherd, my servant David, and he shall feed them: he shall feed them and be their shepherd. And I, the Lord, will be their God, and my servant David shall be prince among them. I am the Lord; I have spoken. (Ezek. 34:20–24)

So often in the middle of Israel's despair, when their trouble has been troubled further by wicked and selfish leaders, God makes promises that, no matter how they are received at the moment, find their full fulfillment only in Jesus. Think of how the Gospel of Matthew begins: "The book of the genealogy of Jesus Christ, the son of David, the son of Abraham" (Matt. 1:1). All of the promises about David's unending kingdom are fulfilled in Jesus. John declares, through the words of Jesus, that Jesus is the promised good shepherd:

> I am the good shepherd. The good shepherd lays down his life for the sheep. He who is a hired hand and not a shepherd, who does not own the sheep, sees the wolf coming and leaves the sheep

and flees, and the wolf snatches them and scatters them. He flees because he is a hired hand and cares nothing for the sheep. I am the good shepherd. I know my own and my own know me, just as the Father knows me and I know the Father; and I lay down my life for the sheep. And I have other sheep that are not of this fold. I must bring them also, and they will listen to my voice. So there will be one flock, one shepherd. For this reason the Father loves me, because I lay down my life that I may take it up again. (John 10:11–17)

Ultimately, what the people of old needed, and what we need as well, was a better human shepherd. Jesus, the God-man, is that better shepherd. Yes, the human shepherds of Israel were derelict in their duties. They loved themselves more than they loved God and his people. Yes, it would have greatly benefited the people of God if they had been led by godly leaders. But, because of the presence and power of sin, what humanity needs is a shepherd who would lay down his life for the redemption of his sheep. Be glad today that Jesus is that shepherd. He laid down his life so that you might have life forever.

---— REFLECTION ---—

How might Jesus be seeking to shepherd you right now? How can you submit more fully to his care?

---— PRAYER ---—

Heavenly Father, I rest secure in your promise of a good shepherd. I delight to know that you have promised one who will tend to his people with attentive care and love. Even more so, you have provided that shepherd in the person of Jesus, the heir of David and King of the world! Thank you for providing one who would lay down his life for his sheep, so that I may be reconciled to you. I pray in his name, amen.

DECEMBER 14
DANIEL 7:1–18

*The entire biblical story marches toward
the coming of the Son of Man.*

If you were to introduce Jesus to someone who had never heard of him before, what would you say? The central character and eternal hope of the biblical narrative is Jesus. All of the promises of God balance on his shoulders. Everything that we need is supplied in and through him. He is the hope of the Old Testament and the conquering hero of the New Testament. By grace our little stories are embedded in his great victorious narrative. The Bible is the biography of Jesus. It is the revelation of his character, power, wisdom, holiness, and redeeming work. At the center of all the promises of God is the promised Son.

Daniel 7–12 records the apocalyptic visions of Daniel. These visions are meant to assure the people of God at that time, as well as us, that despite persecution and hardship God still reigns, his plan still marches on, and his promises are still trustworthy:

> there came one like a son of man,
> and he came to the Ancient of Days
>   and was presented before him.
> And to him was given dominion
>   and glory and a kingdom,
> that all peoples, nations, and languages
>   should serve him;
> his dominion is an everlasting dominion,
>   which shall not pass away,
> and his kingdom one
>   that shall not be destroyed. (Dan. 7:13–14)

God sits on his holy and royal throne as the sole ruler of the universe he created. The one like a son of man is presented to him. This description of Jesus is a reminder to us that he is fully God and fully man. After Jesus is presented to the Father, God grants him everlasting dominion over all humanity and a kingdom that will never be destroyed. This is a gloriously encouraging and hope-infusing description of the one in whom you have placed your hope.

It is important that we think of Jesus not only as the sacrificial Lamb but also as the risen, ascended, and reigning King. What happens after the resurrection is very important. Jesus ascends on a cloud to be seated at the right hand of the Father to reign forever and ever (Acts 1:9). His reign is not a future promise, but a present reality. We have hope right here, right now because his reign guarantees that he has the power and authority to deliver to us everything that his work on earth purchased for us. His present reign guarantees that he will someday usher in the final kingdom, where we will be blessed with uninterrupted peace and righteousness forever.

Today, celebrate the reign of your Savior and go out and live with courage and hope.

---- REFLECTION ----

In what ways is Jesus's royal status demonstrated even in his humble birth in Bethlehem?

---- PRAYER ----

Ancient of Days, you are great and glorious. All power and authority belong to you. And yet you have given your kingdom to your Son, one like a son of man, that all peoples, nations, and languages should serve him. I praise you for including me in that kingdom, that I might forever praise the one who lives and reigns even now. I pray in the name of this great King, Jesus, amen.

DECEMBER 15
MATTHEW 2:1-12

In Jesus, God has fulfilled the greatest promise of all: his promise that a Messiah was coming.

The book of Matthew provides us with one of the most familiar accounts in the Bible of the birth and infancy of Jesus:

> Now after Jesus was born in Bethlehem of Judea in the days of Herod the king, behold, wise men from the east came to Jerusalem, saying, "Where is he who has been born king of the Jews? For we saw his star when it rose and have come to worship him." When Herod the king heard this, he was troubled, and all Jerusalem with him; and assembling all the chief priests and scribes of the people, he inquired of them where the Christ was to be born. They told him, "In Bethlehem of Judea, for so it is written by the prophet:
>
> 'And you, O Bethlehem, in the land of Judah,
>   are by no means least among the rulers of Judah;
> for from you shall come a ruler
>   who will shepherd my people Israel.'" (Matt. 2:1–6)

When Herod went to Old Testament scholars to inquire where the promised Messiah was to be born, they had no problem answering. They immediately quoted Micah 5:2. The promise of God, made through the prophet Micah many generations before, was specific—down to the exact town in which he would be born. The King of kings wouldn't have a regal birth in a royal palace in Jerusalem, with an adoring court at his cradle. No, the hope of the world would be born in the town of Bethlehem to a mother and father who were far from the royalty of that day.

Every detail of Jesus's birth was part of God's plan before the foundations of the earth were set in place. So the promises and prophecies of his birth were detailed and specific. God is not like a fortune teller, delivering a safe, generic prediction. No, these promises were made by the Lord of heaven and earth, who rules everything, everywhere, all the time. You see, the promises of God are only as good as the extent of his sovereignty, because he can guarantee the delivery of his promises only in situations over which he has rule. Because he rules everything, everywhere, all of the time, however, his promises are specific and rock solid.

The specificity of God's promise about where the Messiah would be born is a picture of how infinitely confident God is in his own ability to do whatever he has said he will do, wherever he said he will do it, and whenever he knows the time is right. You can bank on and build your life upon the promises of God. He has the power, willingness, and authority to do everything he has promised to do. It is so good to know today that you can absolutely trust that he will do what he has said he will do.

REFLECTION

Are there areas in your life concerning which you find it difficult to trust God's sovereign promises? How does Jesus's birth allow you to trust him in all things?

PRAYER

Indeed, O God, how good it is to know that you are absolutely trustworthy! You have promised in your word that you will do marvelous things—and I know that you will do what you have said you will do! Thank you for sending your Son at just the right time in order to accomplish your perfect sovereign will for this world that you have made. Thank you for claiming me as his own, as your own. In his name I come, amen.

DECEMBER 16
MATTHEW 3:1–17

*Jesus is the eternal Son of the Father who came
to give his life as a ransom for many.*

I remember the first time we visited Northern Ireland. As we drove on those ribbon roads, I was in awe of the beauty all around me. There really were forty shades of green. White sheep made it look as though God had painted polka dots on the ground. White limestone cliffs dropped down to the sea. The rain seemed to enhance, rather than detract from, the created glories we were trying our best to take in. I thought, "I don't care if it's raining. Sometimes you need to stop, pause your journey for a moment, and take in the beauty." The north coast of Ireland displays a bit of God's glory for his creatures to relish.

The beginning of Matthew presents us with a majestic one-time moment in history that you shouldn't run past in your desire to complete your daily Bible reading. God has recorded and preserved it for you because he wants it to leave you in gratitude and awe. And that awe is meant to capture your heart with such force that it changes the way you think about who you are and how you live your life. This scene, the baptism of Jesus, is in the Bible because God loves you:

> Then Jesus came from Galilee to the Jordan to John, to be baptized by him. John would have prevented him, saying, "I need to be baptized by you, and do you come to me?" But Jesus answered him, "Let it be so now, for thus it is fitting for us to fulfill all righteousness." Then he consented. And when Jesus was baptized, immediately he went up from the water, and behold, the heavens were opened to him, and he saw the Spirit of God descending like

a dove and coming to rest on him; and behold, a voice from heaven said, "This is my beloved Son, with whom I am well pleased." (Matt. 3:13–17)

Pay careful attention to the tenderhearted and loving beauty of the voice from heaven: "This is my beloved Son, with whom I am well pleased." With these words you are invited to witness the eternal love relationship between the Father and the Son. Who is Jesus? He is not just a man from Bethlehem; he is the loved and pleasing Son of the Father. But there is something else here. Why would Jesus need to submit to the baptism of repentance? He had no sin. But here Jesus nevertheless humbly and willingly identified with those for whom he had come to suffer and die. In the beginning of his life he identified with them, and at the end of his earthly life he took their sin on his shoulders. Here is your Jesus. He is the Son of the Father and the Lamb of sacrifice. He's the grace of God in the flesh.

REFLECTION

How can your celebration of Christ's advent deepen your grasp and appreciation of God's love for you in Christ?

PRAYER

Triune God, when I attempt to comprehend your perfect love from all eternity, my mind cannot grasp the depths of this reality. I am left in wonder over your love for one another. And I am awestruck that you would extend this love to sinners such as I—at the great cost of Jesus's willingness to identify himself with sinners through his baptism and death. Thank you for this amazing truth. In Jesus's name, amen.

DECEMBER 17
MATTHEW 20:20–28

Jesus, the King of kings who came not to be served but to serve and give his life as a ransom for many, shows us what his kingdom is like.

It is clear that our culture is obsessed with greatness. The people who are our heroes have lots of power, stacks of money, piles of achievements, tons of human acclaim, warehouses of possessions, multiple houses, and fleets of luxury vehicles. We love to watch videos that take us into their homes or let us see their amazing cars. We like feats of power, and we look up to people who take control. Our heroes are kingdom builders who have accomplished and acquired much, and who have crowds of people around them to serve their purposes. We often watch the coronation of another business leader, entertainment star, sports champion, or national king and silently think, "If only."

But the King of kings is unlike any earthly king. The Lord Creator and sovereign of the universe did not invade the earth he created so that he could set up an earthly kingdom and be served. No, his coming, his life, and his death displayed the ultimate humble, self-sacrificing service. What was Jesus's experience on earth? An inauspicious birth and poverty of life. Mocking and rejection. An unjust and violent arrest and trial. Horrific suffering on the cross. Jesus poured out his life—not for his own power and earthly fame, but for the eternal salvation of all who put their trust in him. If this is the way of the King, then why would we think that the call and culture of his kingdom would be any different?

In Matthew 20 we find the mother of the sons of Zebedee asking Jesus to secure a special place of honor for her sons in his kingdom. Here is Jesus's response:

"You do not know what you are asking. Are you able to drink the cup that I am to drink?" They said to him, "We are able." He said to them, "You will drink my cup, but to sit at my right hand and at my left is not mine to grant, but it is for those for whom it has been prepared by my Father." And when the ten heard it, they were indignant at the two brothers. But Jesus called them to him and said, "You know that the rulers of the Gentiles lord it over them, and their great ones exercise authority over them. It shall not be so among you. But whoever would be great among you must be your servant, and whoever would be first among you must be your slave, even as the Son of Man came not to be served but to serve, and to give his life as a ransom for many." (Matt. 20:22–28)

It is vital to understand that God's kingdom is an upside-down kingdom, where the path to greatness is via humble service. Because of the greatness of Jesus's service, we have hope in this life and the one to come.

REFLECTION

Are there ways in which you are attempting to be great in the eyes of the world? How can Christ's birth and ministry reorient your priorities in light of his service?

PRAYER

I love your kingdom, Lord. I love how you rule over all time and space and yet make your reign most evident in this world through the suffering band of fallen saints known as the church. Make your people to follow after your example of service, not notoriety. May we love and sacrifice for others, just as you have done for us. I pray in your name, amen.

DECEMBER 18
LUKE 1:26–55

*We sing today—and we will sing for all of
eternity—songs of the grace of Jesus.*

God hardwired us to sing. We sing spiritual songs, political songs, love songs, protest songs, happy songs, funeral songs, painful songs, and joyful songs. Once our five-year-old granddaughter told us, "I made up a song about kitties." We said, "Let's hear it," and off she went, singing the song she had made up on the fly. Composing and singing songs are quintessentially human. Our songs are expressions of the emotions and values of our hearts. Our songs reveal more about us than we might think.

So, when we read Scripture, we should slow down and pay attention to its songs. These songs are meant to focus our hearts, instruct us in the ways of the Lord, motivate our joy, and put words to our worship. One of Scripture's most wonderful songs was composed by Mary. An angel had visited her and announced that she would give birth to the promised Messiah. When Mary visited her cousin Elizabeth, Mary sang this song:

My soul magnifies the Lord,
    and my spirit rejoices in God my Savior,
for he has looked on the humble estate of his servant.
    For behold, from now on all generations will call me blessed;
for he who is mighty has done great things for me,
    and holy is his name.
And his mercy is for those who fear him
    from generation to generation.
He has shown strength with his arm;
    he has scattered the proud in the thoughts of their hearts;

he has brought down the mighty from their thrones
>   and exalted those of humble estate;
> he has filled the hungry with good things,
>   and the rich he has sent away empty.
> He has helped his servant Israel,
>   in remembrance of his mercy,
> as he spoke to our fathers,
>   to Abraham and to his offspring forever. (Luke 1:46–55)

Notice Mary's humility. She knows she didn't earn the blessing of giving birth to the Messiah. She is but a humble servant, blessed with the favor of the Lord. Then notice how she speaks of her Lord. He is mighty in authority and strength, and also tenderhearted in mercy. He deals with sin, while meeting the needs of his people. He remembers and keeps his covenant promises. Those promises will find their final fulfillment in the life, death, and resurrection of the little one in Mary's womb. Holy is his name.

Mary's gospel song has been preserved for us so that this joyful and Godward expression of her heart would be the song of our hearts as well.

REFLECTION

Are there lines or phrases from Mary's song that seem especially relevant or precious to you in this stage of life? If so, use them to magnify the name of your Savior and Lord, Jesus Christ.

PRAYER

My spirit rejoices in you, my God and my Savior. Indeed, your name is holy, and your mercy is for those who fear you from generation to generation. You have exalted the humble and filled the hungry with good things. O Lord, thank you for giving us every good thing in Jesus. In his name I come before you, amen.

DECEMBER 19
LUKE 2:22–38

Jesus is humanity's great fault line; every person's eternal fate is set by the rejection or acceptance of him. There is no neutral ground.

When Mary and Joseph took young Jesus to the temple, they didn't know that Simeon, a righteous man, would be waiting there for him. The Holy Spirit had told Simeon that he would not die before he saw the "Lord's Christ" (2:26). Simeon took Jesus in his arms. What an amazing scene. Imagine being chosen by God to hold the young Messiah in your arms! As he held Jesus, Simeon spoke these words:

> Lord, now you are letting your servant depart in peace,
>   according to your word;
> for my eyes have seen your salvation
>   that you have prepared in the presence of all peoples,
> a light for revelation to the Gentiles,
>   and for glory to your people Israel. (Luke 2:29–32)

After Simeon spoke his words of blessing, worship, and prophecy, he turned to Mary and said, "Behold, this child is appointed for the fall and rising of many in Israel, and for a sign that is opposed (and a sword will pierce through your own soul also), so that thoughts from many hearts may be revealed" (Luke 2:34–35). These would have been hard and confusing words for the young mother of the Messiah to hear.

Simeon captured the inescapable truth about the identity, person, and work of Jesus. When you are presented with the truth of Christ's birth, God's declaration of who he is, the testimony of his miracles and ministry, and his own self-testimony, you cannot be neutral about Jesus. Spiritually, you either rise or fall with your response to him. It is not enough to say he was a good prophet and teacher. You either say he is the Messiah Savior and bow before him and cry out for his grace, or you reject him and your need for his grace. You either worship him, or you mock him. You either confess your need for him, or you turn in independence away from him. The great line that divides humanity is not political, economic, social, or ethnic. No, the great fault line is Jesus.

When Simeon told Mary that a sword would pierce her soul, he was, of course, speaking of Calvary, when Mary would watch as a spear pierced the side of her Messiah son. What agony awaited this young mother.

The cross of Jesus either is your hope in this life and the one to come, or it represents the death of a man you do not love and do not need. There is no neutrality in the shadow of the cross.

So, today, what will you do with Jesus? Will you bow in worship and gratitude, or will you take life in your own hands and walk away?

REFLECTION

As we begin this final week of Advent, who do you say Jesus is? And what difference to your life does your answer make?

PRAYER

Great is your salvation, O Lord of heaven and earth! What a glorious salvation you have prepared and brought to fruition through the merciful work of your Son, our Savior, the Lord Jesus. He is indeed a light for revelation to the Gentiles and for glory to your people Israel. In him you are making all things new, including me. Thank you for this grace. In Jesus's name I pray, amen.

DECEMBER 20
JOHN 1:1–18

Jesus is the glory of God in the flesh.

Luella and I split our time between Philadelphia and Southern California because we have children and grandchildren on both coasts. When we are on the West Coast, we see gorgeous sunsets. One evening, as we were leaving our son's house, I was stopped in my tracks by a sunset of incredible glory. The beauty painted across the heavens captivated me. I stood silent, enthralled by this natural display. I wanted to capture the moment, so I got out my phone and started taking pictures, but all I got was disappointment. None of my pictures came close to capturing the glory that I was taking in. Soon the sunset glory began to shift and fade, and before long it was gone. For a brief moment, God had poured glory down on us. What we saw that night was a brief, fading reminder of his eternal glory. Reigning over heaven and earth is a God of indescribable glory. He graces us with glimpses of his glory so that we will be in awe of his presence and offer him the worship of our hearts.

We find a glory display in the beginning of the Gospel of John that is infinitely brighter and more beautiful than any sunset. John captures in words a moment in history when God displayed his glory like never before. Words pile upon words as John records God's stunning glory on earth, for human eyes to see:

The Word became flesh and dwelt among us, and we have seen his glory, glory as of the only Son from the Father, full of grace and truth. (John bore witness about him, and cried out, "This was he of whom I said, 'He who comes after me ranks before me, because he was before me.'") For from his fullness we have all received, grace upon grace. For the law was given through Moses; grace and truth came through Jesus Christ. No one has ever seen God; God the only Son, who is at the Father's side, he has made him known. (John 1:14–18)

God has come to earth in the person of Jesus. Like the presence of God in the Old Testament tabernacle, Jesus pitches his tent with us, so we might see his glory. He is the grace of God in the flesh. He is truth. He is the final fulfillment of all the Old Testament's redemptive promises. Just as the Law of Moses reveals God's character and his righteous requirements, so Jesus reveals to us the magnitude of his mercy. The Son of God has come to earth because God wants to be known by us.

All of history had been marching to this moment. A sin-broken world had been longing for this one to come. Fully man and fully God, Jesus would do what we could never do for ourselves: make a way, in his life and death, for us to be recognized by God. Stop today for a moment and take in the glory.

──────────── REFLECTION ────────────

Think of all the ways that God's glory was revealed in the Old Testament tabernacle. How does Jesus fulfill and exceed all those Old Testament elements?

──────────── PRAYER ────────────

O majestic Lord, how great is your glory, and the glory of your Son! What wonder that he would take on human flesh to dwell among sinners. What glorious revelation of your character and righteous requirements in his perfect life and sacrificial death. May I never lose a sense of wonder and awe at the gospel of your Son. He is my only comfort, my only hope. I ask this in his name, amen.

DECEMBER 21
JOHN 3:1–21

God's generosity culminates in the gift of his Son, Jesus.

The Bible records the best generosity story that has ever been penned in human language. God is the great giver of good things, and the biblical narrative records his generosity over and over again. The creation account shows us his generosity as he places Adam and Eve in a beautiful garden where they have everything they need. In generosity, right after the entrance of sin into the world, God promises to fix what sin has broken. God generously makes his covenant with Abraham, through whom all the nations on earth will be blessed. He is generous in delivering his people out of slavery and giving them his law so that they will thrive. He generously provides manna for them in the wilderness when they aren't able to provide for themselves. He generously provides the promised land so they can grow and thrive as a nation. In generosity, he chooses to dwell with them in the tabernacle; his presence is always with them. In the face of their rebellion, God generously sends prophet after prophet to warn his people and call them back to him.

If you pay attention as you read your Bible, you will see that the generosity of the King of kings is without end. One particular verse captures God's generosity and its final culmination. This verse may be the most famous and well-known of all Bible verses: "For God so loved the world, that he gave his only Son, that whoever believes in him should not perish but have eternal life" (John 3:16).

I am convinced that this passage not only points us to the ultimate gift of gifts, Jesus, but it also summarizes the redemptive story up until this point. We can summarize the redemptive story with these nine words: "For God so loved the world that he gave."

The entire biblical story is about a God who gives his creatures what they do not know they need, what they often do not want, and what they could never earn or do for themselves—but which they cannot live without. As we read the Bible, it becomes clear that nothing can keep God from giving. Even in the face of his people's rebellion and idolatry, he continues to give. His generosity is inexhaustible and without limit.

God's generosity reached its crescendo with the gift of Jesus. Every gift he had given pointed to this final gift. In this gift, we get forgiveness, reconciliation, and the transformation of our hearts. In all of God's giving, there is no gift like Jesus.

God is still showering down his generosity on you. He blesses you every day with his presence, promises, power, and grace. He gives to you through his word and his church. Your life—right here, right now, and into the future—rests on God's willingness to keep on giving. It is an amazing grace that we are the objects of such unending generosity.

REFLECTION

Why is God's gift to you of Jesus such a precious gift? How should we respond to the giving of such a valuable gift?

PRAYER

My God, I thank you for the richness of your generosity to your people! I have done nothing to deserve such a benevolent Lord and King! You bless me in so many ways, each and every day. You delight me with your presence. You move me with your power. You shower me with your grace. I extol your name for the supreme gift of Jesus, your Son, who will be mine forever because of his unbreakable commitment to me. I thank you in his name, amen.

DECEMBER 22
JOHN 20:24–31

Your Bible is the biography of Jesus. On his shoulders the hope of humanity rests, both in this life and in the one to come.

I remember my very first Bible. Owning it made me feel so grown up and truly part of the spiritual community that I was being raised in. It was a leather-bound, loose-leaf Bible, which allowed you to insert pages for note-taking. As a little boy I was proud of this book, but I had no idea what life-transforming glories it contained. I knew the creation narrative and other well-known Bible stories, but little else. If you had asked me what the Bible was about or why God had given it to us, I'm not sure what I would have answered. What is the central theme of your Bible? What is the unifying cord that holds every part of it together? Why did God go to all the effort over so many years to record and preserve his word for us? How does God intend for us to use our Bibles? Can you describe the Bible in a single sentence? How much do you value Scripture?

Near the end of his Gospel, John recounts the last moments of Jesus's life on earth. He then pauses to tell us why he wrote what he wrote. John's description of his purpose for writing his Gospel is incredibly important—not only for understanding the importance of this Gospel but also for understanding who you are, what you need, and how God will meet that need with his grace. But there is more. John's statement gets at the reason for *every* part of the word of God. It exposes God's central mission for his revelation to us. In fact, John's purpose statement for his Gospel is by far the best way to understand what your Bible is meant to do for you and in you:

> Now Jesus did many other signs in the presence of the disciples, which are not written in this book; but these are written so that

you may believe that Jesus is the Christ, the Son of God, and that by believing you may have life in his name. (John 20:30–31)

The first thing you learn about John's Gospel and your Bible is that neither was intended to give you an exhaustive history of the redemptive narrative and its central character, Jesus. What you have in your Bible is selective history, with all of the necessary explanatory notes. The purpose of Scripture is to point you to the one who carries fallen humanity's hope so that you will embrace your need of him, put your trust in him, and receive the greatest gift ever given: *life in his name*. Your Bible was written with a Jesus-elevating, salvation-producing purpose. It is more than history, poetry, and wisdom. The Bible is the biography of Jesus, who is the way, the truth, and the life.

---- REFLECTION ----

Why does believing in Jesus lead to "life in his name"? How can you be sure personally that you enjoy this life even now?

---- PRAYER ----

Holy God, may I accept and receive your word for what it truly is! May I not bend it for my own purposes, but instead may I accept its testimony of Jesus. May I truly know and believe that he is your Son and anointed one, the God and King over all. Increase my faith and belief in him, and bring me safely to the eternal rest you have won for me in him. Through him is this possible as I pray, amen.

DECEMBER 23
PHILIPPIANS 2:1–18

*Our hope in this life and the one to come rests on
the humiliation and exaltation of the Son.*

It's important to confess that we love being exalted and dislike being humbled. None of us enjoys moments when we are proven to be less than others, and we revel in situations where we are elevated. Acclaim, respect, appreciation, power, control, and position are seductive idols for us all. We hate to be embarrassed or shown to be weak. Being humbled is hard for us.

Philippians 2 makes it clear that Jesus is not like us:

Have this mind among yourselves, which is yours in Christ Jesus, who, though he was in the form of God, did not count equality with God a thing to be grasped, but emptied himself, by taking the form of a servant, being born in the likeness of men. And being found in human form, he humbled himself by becoming obedient to the point of death, even death on a cross. Therefore God has highly exalted him and bestowed on him the name that is above every name, so that at the name of Jesus every knee should bow, in heaven and on earth and under the earth, and every tongue confess that Jesus Christ is Lord, to the glory of God the Father. (Phil. 2:5–11)

As the apostle Paul calls the Philippian believers to live a life of humility, he encourages them to have the mind of Christ. Jesus, equal with the Father and the Holy Spirit in divine majesty, sovereignty, holiness, and power, willingly humbled himself. Paul assures us that Jesus wasn't humbled, but rather willingly humbled himself. What did his willing humiliation look like?

He emptied himself.
He took on the form of a servant.
He took on human likeness.
He became obedient, even to death on a cross.

Jesus didn't come to earth in a display of divine splendor. From the manger to homelessness, mockery, rejection, and public crucifixion, Jesus's life was a portrait of humility. He came to be not an earthly monarch but a sacrificial Lamb. Our justification and adoption as the children of God rest on the willing humiliation of the Son. We should be his humble and willing children. But, thankfully, our hope rests not on our willingness but on his.

Paul doesn't stop with Jesus's willing humiliation; he also points us to Christ's exaltation. Humble Jesus now sits at the right hand of the Father as the reigning King. The final defeat of sin and death and the delivery of the final kingdom of peace and righteousness rest on the exaltation of the Son. There will be a day when every knee will bow and every tongue will confess that Jesus is, in fact, Lord.

Be thankful for the willing humiliation and great exaltation of the Son. The sacrificial Lamb is now a reigning King. Hallelujah!

--- REFLECTION ---

What difference does it make that the same Jesus humbled at the cross is now exalted on high?

--- PRAYER ---

Lord, even now I bow before the throne of Jesus. Even now I confess that he is Lord, master and ruler of all things, king of the universe. And yet what humility he has displayed! What tender love to stoop so low, even to die on behalf of me and all his chosen people. May I display that same sort of humility in all that I do. In Jesus's name, amen.

DECEMBER 24
HEBREWS 1:1–14

How would you describe Jesus, the one on whom you have hung your hope in this life and the one to come?

No book of the Bible begins as Hebrews does. It's as though the writer of Hebrews invites you into the divine theater and ushers you to a great seat. As the orchestra swells, he pulls back the curtain, and a bright and shining light of glory bursts forth from the stage. He says, "Here is your Savior":

Long ago, at many times and in many ways, God spoke to our fathers by the prophets, but in these last days he has spoken to us by his Son, whom he appointed the heir of all things, through whom also he created the world. He is the radiance of the glory of God and the exact imprint of his nature, and he upholds the universe by the word of his power. After making purification for sins, he sat down at the right hand of the Majesty on high, having become as much superior to angels as the name he has inherited is more excellent than theirs.

For to which of the angels did God ever say,

> "You are my Son,
>   today I have begotten you"? . . .

But of the Son he says,

> "Your throne, O God, is forever and ever,
>   the scepter of uprightness is the scepter of your
>   kingdom.
> You have loved righteousness and hated wickedness;

>   therefore God, your God, has anointed you
>   with the oil of gladness beyond your companions."
>   (Heb. 1:1–5, 8–9)

This portrait of the Savior is majestic and multifaceted. It is meant not only to deepen and clarify your understanding of the second person of the Trinity, but to change you, to deepen your understanding of who you are as God's child. Sometimes such glory prompts you to stop, be silent, behold, and worship. Hebrews 1 offers us an account of this kind of glory.

So, who is Jesus? He is God's final revelation to us. In him we see the full radiance of God's glory, because he shares God's exact nature. Jesus not only created the world, but he is the one who holds the creation together by his infinite power. Jesus is the only one who has the power to purify us from sin. He is God the Father's beloved Son, who now sits at his right hand. Jesus is majestic in glory and brimming with redeeming grace. He reigns over his creation for the sake of his own. There is no one more worthy of your hope. There is no one more worthy of your trust. There is no one more deserving of your worship. Today, and all the days that follow, we bow before the majesty of our Savior King and offer our whole hearts and lives to him.

REFLECTION

How can your celebration of this Christmas season lead to greater worship of and devotion to King Jesus?

PRAYER

Jesus, I am stunned by your glory. You created the world and now hold it together. You use your purifying power to cleanse your people from sin. You rule in gladness and righteousness. You are majestic and gracious. All I can do is worship you with all that I am. In your name I do so, amen.

DECEMBER 25
REVELATION 12:1-17

Your hope in this life and the one to come was secured in the ultimate battle that took place at the birth of Jesus.

All of history marched toward one decisive event. The entire plan of God, the entire hope of humanity, and the entire work of redemption balanced on this moment. It had been prophesied. It had been promised. The reputation of the Almighty rested on whether it would happen or not. Could the Lord of lords fulfill his promise of the birth of his Son? If the Son would not be born, there could be no righteous life lived in our place, no death to free us from sin's penalty, no victorious resurrection, and no ascension to the Father to reign and intercede on our behalf. There could be no redemption and no hope.

Revelation 12 captures the battle that occurred at this pivotal moment in history:

> And a great sign appeared in heaven: a woman clothed with the sun, with the moon under her feet, and on her head a crown of twelve stars. She was pregnant and was crying out in birth pains and the agony of giving birth. And another sign appeared in heaven: behold, a great red dragon, with seven heads and ten horns, and on his heads seven diadems. His tail swept down a third of the stars of heaven and cast them to the earth. And the dragon stood before the woman who was about to give birth, so that when she bore her child he might devour it. She gave birth to a male child, one who is to rule all the nations with a rod of iron, but her child was caught up to God and to his throne, and the woman fled into the wilderness, where she has a place prepared by God, in which she is to be nourished for 1,260 days. (Rev. 12:1–6)

This is a picture of the great spiritual battle that began with the birth of Jesus. Israel is the pregnant woman, Jesus is the male child, and Satan is the great red dragon. Satan and the forces of darkness would have done anything to end the life of the promised Son.

The end of the reign of evil on earth began with the birth of Jesus. Later Satan would be defeated at Christ's temptation, he would be defeated on the cross, and he would be defeated by the empty tomb. Jesus was victorious on our behalf and now reigns in glory. His reign guarantees the end of sin and death and an eternity of peace and righteousness for all who believe. The dragon is defeated. The Son reigns. Hallelujah!

REFLECTION

Why did Jesus need to be born as a human in order to defeat the dragon?

PRAYER

Lord God, I rest in the mighty victory of your Son, Jesus Christ! I praise you for your great power in defeating sin and Satan at the cross, and with hope I look forward to the day when Satan will be banished forever. I delight in the reign of Christ, which guarantees an eternity of peace and righteousness. I pray in his name, amen.

Everyday Gospel Book and Bible

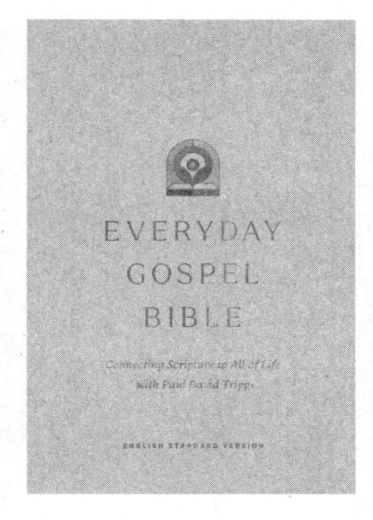

In the *Everyday Gospel* devotional, Paul David Tripp guides readers through the entire Bible in a year, helping them connect the transforming power of Scripture to their everyday life. The *ESV Everyday Gospel Bible* features the same daily devotions embedded within the full ESV Bible text, along with theologically rich articles, applicational sidebars, and book introductions.

Order now at **PaulTripp.com** or **Crossway.org**.

PAUL TRIPP MINISTRIES

Paul Tripp Ministries is a not-for-profit organization connecting the transforming power of Jesus Christ to everyday life. Supported by generous donors, they make much of Paul's gospel teaching freely available online, on podcasts, across social media, and in the Paul Tripp app.

PaulTripp.com

/pdtripp   @paultripp   @paultrippquotes

@pauldavidtripp   /add/pauldavidtripp   /in/paul-david-tripp/

Google Play   App Store